All About Germany

100+ Amazing Facts You Didn't Know Before

Bandana Ojha

All rights reserved. This book or any portion thereof may not be reproduced or used in any manner without the express written permission of the author.
Copyright © 2022 By the author.

Introduction

Filled with up-to-date information, fascinating & fun facts this book " All About GERMANY: 100+ Amazing & Interesting Facts You Didn't Know Before" is the best book for kids to find out more about "The Land of Poets and Thinkers". This book would satisfy the children's curiosity and help them to understand why Germany is one of the most popular member states of the European Union and what makes it different from other European nations. This book gives a story, history & explores the country's best cuisine, architecture, fashion, art, language, people, places, national symbols, and many more. It is a fun and fascinating way for young readers to find out more interesting facts. This is a great chance for every kid to expand their knowledge about Germany and impress family and friends with all "discovered and never knew before" amazing facts.

Germany officially the "Federal Republic of Germany", is a country in Central Europe.

Germany borders more countries than any other state in Europe. It has 9 neighboring counties- Denmark to the north, Netherlands, Belgium, Luxemburg, and France to the west, Switzerland and Austria to the south, and the Czech Republic and Poland to the east.

It is the second most populous country in Europe after Russia, and the most populous member state of the European Union.

Germany is the 5th largest country in Europe after Ukraine, France, Sweden, and Spain.

About 1/3rd of Germany is covered by forests

The nick name of Germany is "Land of Poets and Thinkers" because its scientists, writers and philosophers have played a major role in the development of Western thoughts.

The official language of Germany is German.

National founder of Germany is Otto Von Bismarck.

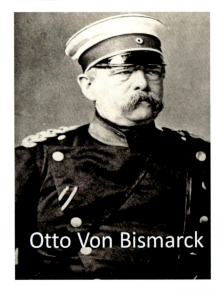

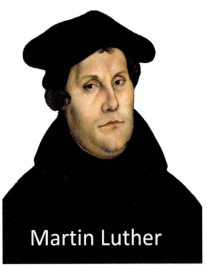

National hero of Germany is Martin Luther.

On February 2nd 962 AD, Germany was first recognized as a region. On January 18th, 1871, Germany became a unified state and on October 3rd, 1990, East and West Germany were united to form the current Federal Republic of Germany.

National Day of Germany is October 3rd. It is also called German Unity Day.

National Flag is "The Flag of German".

It is a tricolor consisting of three equal horizontal bands displaying the national colors of Germany: black, red, and gold.

National Coat of Arms is "The Coat of Arms of German."

The coat of arms of Germany displays a black eagle on a yellow shield. The coat of arms is like those of the flag of Germany - black, red, and gold. It is the oldest existing state symbol in Europe and is one of the oldest emblems in the world.

National Anthem is "Deutschlandlied".

National Currency is **Euro**. Before Euro, the **Deutsche Mark** was used as their currency.

National Colors are Black, red, and gold.

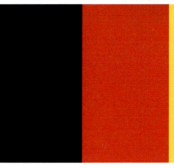

National Tree is Royal Oak Quercus.

National Bird is Black Eagle.

National Dish is Sauerbraten.

A Sauerbraten is a traditional heavily marinated roasted meat. It can be prepared from a variety of meats, most often from beef, but also from lamb, mutton, and pork.

Sauerbraten recipes vary by region, each adding their own touches. Some regions use just vinegar, some just wine and others use a combination of both, which is the most common.

National drink is Lager.

National Flower is Cyani flower.

National Fruit is Apple.

Nationality of Germany is German.

The capital of Germany is Berlin, which is in the northeast part of the country.

Berlin is the largest city of Germany. Berlin is nine times larger than Paris and has more bridges than Venice.

Before the reunification, Bonn was the capital of West Germany while East Berlin was the capital of the East Germany.

Before Berlin, there have been many capital cities of Germany including Aachen, Regensburg, Frankfurt-am-Main, Nuremberg, Weimar, and Bonn.

National dance of Germany is Schuhplattler.

National dress of Germany is Dirndls.

National monument of Germany is Cologne Cathedral.

National sports of Germany is Football

There is no official motto of Germany, but Unity, justice and freedom are commonly used.

National poet of Germany is Johann Wolfgang Von Goethe.

He was a poet, playwright, novelist, scientist, statesman, theatre director, and critic. He is widely regarded as the greatest and most influential writer in the German language, his work having a profound and wide-ranging influence on Western literary, political, and philosophical thought from the late 18th century to the present day.

Religion of Germany is Christianity.

National airline of Germany is Lufthansa.

National instrument of Germany is Lute

National Museum of Germany is Germanisches Nationalmuseum.

National library of Germany is "German National Library."

The country's full name is sometimes shortened to the FRG (Federal Republic of Germany) or the BRD (Bundesrepublik Deutschland) in German).

Switzerland, Austria, Luxembourg, and Liechtenstein also have German as the official language

German is spoken by over 100 million people worldwide. It is the third most taught language in the world.

The German alphabet has more than 26 letters. The German pronunciation of these extra letters ä, ö, ü, and ß don't exist in the English language.

There are 35 different dialects of the German language. Because there are so many different dialects in Germany, people may have problems understanding those from different regions - some regional films are even shown with subtitles!

With an elevation of 9,718 ft, Zugspitze is the highest of the Bavarian Alps and the highest point in Germany. The Zugspitze was officially climbed for the first time in 1820.

Zugspitze is one of Germany's top attractions and many tourists visit the mountain top every year.

Germany extends more than 500 miles from north to south and about 400 miles from east to west at its widest.

The longest river of Germany is **Rhine**.

Germany has close to 700 zoological gardens, wildlife parks, aquariums, and animal reserves.

The Berlin Zoo, which opened in 1844, is the oldest in Germany, and claims the most comprehensive collection of species in the world.

There are over 20,000 castles in Germany, most of them being at least 100 years old. Many of these castles were turned into museums and cultural art centers for people to enjoy.

Neuschwanstein fairytale castle, is the most photographed building in the country and one of the most popular tourist attractions in Germany. It. is situated on a rugged hill near Füssen in southwest Bavaria. It was the inspiration for the Sleeping Beauty castles in the Disneyland parks.

Hamburgers got its name from the city of Hamburg, Germany.

In Hamburg, there is a Food Additives Museum dedicated to the emulsifiers, stabilizers, dyes, thickeners, preservatives, and flavorings in our everyday foods. The exhibit explains the history and current landscape of food additives in an informational way.

Germans produce their ubiquitous sausages in almost 1,500 varieties, including Bratwursts and Weisswursts.

More than 800 million currywurst sausages are eaten every year in Germany. The snack is so popular that there's even a museum dedicated to it in Berlin.

Bread is a significant part of German cuisine and German bakeries produce about 600 main types of bread and 1,200 types of pastries and rolls.

German cheeses account for about 22% of all cheese produced in Europe.

In 2012 over 99% of all meat produced in Germany was either pork, chicken, or beef.

Chinese Checkers was invented in Germany in 1892 and was called "Stern-Halma".

Europe's largest train station is in Berlin.

Germany was the first country to implement the Daylight-Saving Time (DST) on April 30, 1916, during World War I.

The longest German word that was ever published is **Donaudampfschifffahrtselektrizitätenhauptbetriebswerkbauunterbeamtengesellschaft.**
It has **79** letters.

Germany is among the top 5 countries with the most Nobel Prize winners. They have 102 of them, including Albert Einstein.

Popular fairy tales, like "Hansel and Gretel," "Snow White," and "Rapunzel," were created by German brothers Jacob and Wilhelm Grimm. The collection of German fairy tales is commonly known in English as Grimm's Fairy Tales.

Germans are incredibly punctual and organized. Munich is the second most punctual airport in the world after Tokyo, and most Germans don't expect to wait around for anything or anyone.

Germany is among the world's largest car manufacturers, and the most popular ones are BMW, Mercedes-Benz, Audi, Porsche, and Volkswagen.

Germany sells around 6 million cars a year.

65% of the highways in Germany have no speed limit and are called the Autobahn.

Germany has the world's narrowest street in the city of Reutlingen called "Spreuerhofstrasse," the street is approximately one foot wide at the narrowest point, and nearly twenty inches wide at the widest.

The German Football Association is called Deutscher Fußball-Bund or DFB.

Germany is one of the most successful national teams in international competitions, having won four World Cups (1954, 1974, 1990, 2014), three European Championships (1972, 1980, 1996), and one Confederations Cup (2017).

They have also been runners-up three times in the European Championships, four times in the World Cup, and a further four third-place finishes at World Cups.

Germany was the last country to host both the summer and winter games in the same year. In 1936, Germany hosted the Summer Games in Berlin and the Winter Games in Garmisch-Partenkirchen. Munich hosted the Summer Games of 1972.

The women's football team is also very successful and has won two FIFA Women's World Cups and a record 8 UEFA European Women's Championships.

The team is governed by the German Football Association (DFB).

There's more soccer fan clubs in Germany than anywhere else in the world.

Gottlieb Daimler and Karl Benz created the first motor-driven vehicles.

Gottlieb Daimler | Karl Benz

People of Germany loves books and around 94,000 titles of books are published every year.

Famous German authors are Bernhard Schlink, W.G Sebald, Franz Kafka and Johann Wolfgang von Goethe.

Frankfurt is the German center of book publishing, where it holds International Frankfurt Book Fair that is one of the most important book events in the world.

Johannes Gutenberg in Germany, introduced printing to Europe with his mechanical movable-type printing press.

 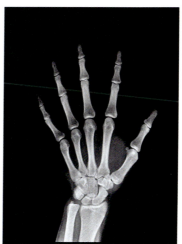

Wilhelm Conrad Roentgen discovered the X-rays in 1895.

The cuckoo clock is invented in Germany in the 17th century.

Some of the world's most famous inventions were created in Germany - the lightbulb, automated calculators, automobiles, insulin, petrol engines, jet engines, and the Walkman and many more.

Gummy Bears was invented by German entrepreneur Hans Riegel, owner of Haribo factory. After seeing trained bears at festivals, Haribo factory created the delicious treat.

The sweet maker, Haribo, runs a scheme where local children can exchange acorns for sweets. Their acorns then get sent to nature reserves to feed animals.

Gum Arabic was the original base ingredient used to produce the gummy bears, hence the name gum or gummy.

The tradition of having a Christmas tree was started in Germany. It was first created during the Renaissance era. Rather than being draped with illuminate lights, the original Christmas tree was decorated with apples, nuts, and other foods.

According to Genesee World Record, A woman named Veronica Seider from Germany, had vision 20 times better than an average person. She can identify people from more than a mile away.

No one in the entire world has been reported so far to possess such astounding vision.

"**Adidas**" was founded by Adolf "Adi" Dassler who made sports shoes in his mother's laundry room in Herzogenaurach, Germany after his return from World War I. In July 1924, his elder brother Rudolf joined the business, which became "Dassler Brothers Shoe Factory".

The brothers split up in 1947 and Rudolf formed a new company that he called Ruda – from Rudolf Dassler, later rebranded as **Puma**, and Adolf forming a company formally registered as Adidas on 18 August 1949.

Adidas is the largest sportswear manufacturer in Europe, and the **second** largest in the world, after Nike. **Puma** is the **third** largest sportswear manufacturer in the world.

Ulm Minster is a Lutheran church, and it is the tallest church in the world. It is in Ulm, State of Baden-Württemberg (Germany).

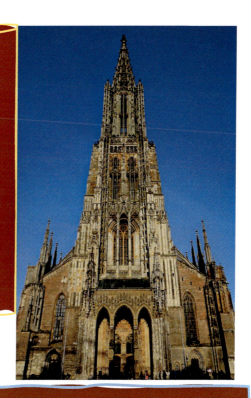

In Germany, Thanksgiving Festival is celebrated in early October.

German people love to travel and spend more on their holidays than any other nation.

The office of the German Chancellor is called the "washing machine" because of its looks - a square shaped building with a round shaped entrance.

It is the world's largest government headquarters (eight times the size of the White House). The nine-story Federal Chancellery was designed by architects Charlotte Franke and Axel Schultes and completed in 2001.

There are more than 380 universities in Germany with over 17,000 study programs.

In an article by the BBC, Germany was the top university in providing global education and supporting international students.

The German school system is extremely well-structured and produces some of the most accomplished students in the world.

When children start school in Germany, they receive something known as a Schultüte – this is a cone of presents that is meant to relieve the stress of the time.

Germans are incredibly punctual and organized. Munich is the second most punctual airport in the world after Tokyo, and most Germans don't expect to wait around for anything or anyone.

The Oktoberfest in Munich is the largest Volksfest in the world with over 6 million visitors annually. Despite the name, the Oktoberfest starts at the end of September until the first weekend in October. The festival has been held since 1810. Visitors enjoy a wide variety of traditional fare such as Hendl, Schweinebraten, Würstl and Knödel.

Please check this out:
Our other best-selling books for kids are-

Know about **Sharks**: Interesting & Amazing Facts That Everyone Should Know

Know About **Whales**: Interesting & Amazing Facts That Everyone Should Know

Know About **Dinosaurs**: Interesting & Amazing Facts That Everyone Should Know

Know About **Kangaroos**: Interesting & Amazing Facts That Everyone Should Know

Know About **Penguins**: Interesting & Amazing Facts That Everyone Should Know

Know About **Dolphins** :100 Interesting & Amazing Facts That Everyone Should Know

Know About **Elephant:** Interesting & Amazing Facts That Everyone Should Know

All About **New York**: Interesting & Amazing Facts That Everyone Should Know

All About **New Jersey**: Interesting & Amazing Facts That Everyone Should Know

All About **Massachusetts**: 100+ Amazing Facts with Pictures

All About **Florida**: Interesting & Amazing Facts That Everyone Should Know

All About **California**: Interesting & Amazing Facts That Everyone Should Know

All About **Arizona**: Interesting & Amazing Facts That Everyone Should Know

All About **Texas**: Interesting & Amazing Facts That Everyone Should Know

All About **Minnesota**: Interesting & Amazing Facts That Everyone Should Know

All About **Illinois**: Interesting & Amazing Facts That Everyone Should Know

All About **New Mexico**: Interesting & Amazing Facts That Everyone Should Know

All About **Canada**: Interesting & Amazing Facts That Everyone Should Know

All About **Australia**: Interesting & Amazing Facts That Everyone Should Know

All About **Italy**: Interesting & Amazing Facts That Everyone Should Know

All About **France**: Interesting & Amazing Facts That Everyone Should Know

All About **Japan**: Interesting & Amazing Facts That Everyone Should Know

100 Amazing **Quiz Q & A About Penguin**: Never Known Before Penguin Facts

Most Popular **Animal Quiz** book for Kids: 100 amazing animal facts

Quiz Book for Kids: Science, History, Geography, Biology, Computer & Information Technology

English **Grammar** for Kids: Most Easy Way to learn English Grammar

Solar System & Space Science- Quiz for Kids: What You Know About Solar System

English **Grammar Practice** Book for elementary kids: 1000+ Practice Questions with Answers

A to Z of **English Tense**

Made in United States
North Haven, CT
13 December 2023